ANGEL OF DEATH

ANGEL OF DEATH

The Shocking True Story of Charles Cullen, the Serial Killer Nurse and the System That Failed To Stop Him

George Mair

Chamberlain Bros.
a member of
Penguin Group (USA) Inc.

Chamberlain Bros.
a member of
Penguin Group (USA) Inc.
375 Hudson Street
New York, NY 10014

An application has been submitted to register this book with the Library of Congress.

ISBN 1-59609-002-2

Printed in the United States of America

1 3 5 7 9 10 8 6 4 2

Book designed by Mike Rivilis.

CONTENTS

INTRODUCTION

The day that the incredible story of Charles Cullen was revealed was one that many in the NY Tri-State area would sooner forget. Cullen's story is the stunning tale of a trusted caregiver, a hospital nurse, who confessed to murdering instead of nurturing. Yet, what seems odd to you and me seemed not at all odd to medical professions and researchers. It was a classic illustration of this kind of serial killer. The big surprise was why it was such a big surprise. We have had serial killers with us for centuries, including the rich, the powerful, and the eccentric. In fact, it should come as no surprise here in the United States, overwhelmingly the serial murder capital of the world. What is horrible to contemplate is that in handing over the care of our helpless loved ones—children, the elderly, the sick—to a caregiver, we could be handing them over to a murderer.

Following the path taken by Charles Cullen, and others like him, may help us to understand this strange and disturbing phenomenon.

1.

THE BIZARRE LIFE OF CAREGIVING MURDERER CHARLES CULLEN

Charles Cullen's case is both unusual and yet in keeping with historic precedence for nurses who kill. Unusual, in that we would never consider a nurse as dangerous or capable of evil but only as a healer who cares for us or our loved ones. In keeping with historic precedence, the grim reality being that killer nurses are more likely to be male than female, as reported by Beatrice Yorker, director of the School of Nursing at San Francisco State University, who says that even though less than 7 percent of nurses in America are male, 33 percent of those who kill are.

In December 2003, Charles Cullen was accused of killing patients out of a sense of mercy to ease their suffering. He astonished authorities, as well as the rest of America and perhaps the world, by claiming to have murdered thirty to forty people in some ten different medical facilities over a sixteen-year period. His confession prompted authorities to launch an investigation looking into "as many as 500 hospital deaths in New Jersey and Pennsylvania."

Many people believe that people like Cullen are playing God, believing they believe they have a right, or, worse yet, a holy mission, to decide who lives and who dies in their little world. The common excuse is the noble act of saving the victim from prolonged suffering. But there is an ego-inflating element as well: the killer has power over another person to do whatever he decides should be done, and that power is his along, to the exclusion of his associates. He can and does kill while his fellow caregivers cannot and do not. That's what makes the killer feel noble and superior, according to experts.

Specifically, Charles Cullen was charged with murdering Florian Gall, a priest—a gesture on Cullen's part, perhaps, that he is superior even to God's own people—in Gall's bed at Somerset Medical Center in Somerset, New Jersey. Cullen allegedly also attempted to murder Jin Kyung Han by injecting her with digoxin, which he stole from hospital supplies. Han recovered from the attempt on her life but, sadly, died several months later from other causes.

Cullen's behavior after he was found out, fired, and arrested may be a clue as to what had been going on in his brain all those years. First of all, he immediately admitted he was guilty and did not want a lawyer to represent him or to contest the charge leveled against him. In fact, he was apparently proud of what he had done, as if it were a righteous deed even if he would be martyred by it, and he craved public recognition. To underscore his pride, after accepting responsibility for the murder of Father Gall he claimed he had killed even more patients—from thirty to forty more! He wanted us to know he was not just a benefactor to the sick but a superbenefactor.

As is usually the case with such ego-driven souls, Charles Cullen did not want to die himself, so he immediately tossed the only bargaining chip he had on the table—namely, he would give details about and clear up those other deaths provided he would not be executed for what he had done.

HOW CHARLES CULLEN BECAME A NURSE

Charles Cullen grew up in a working-class family in New Jersey, one of nine children whose father, a bus driver, died when they were young. He was in high school when he lost his mother in a car accident in 1978, and he dealt with that blow by immediately joining the Navy. He was assigned to submarine duty, but, because of his withdrawn nature and odd behavior, soon became the butt of many of his fellow sailors' ribbing. It got to the point that he attempted suicide, and that lead to his discharge in 1987.

Home in New Jersey, Cullen decided to enroll in Mountainside Hospital School of Nursing in Montclair. He graduated in 1987, married Adrienne Taub, and landed his first nursing job at St. Barnabas Medical Center in Livingston. In time, the couple had two children, and everything seemed all right for a time until the marriage broke up in 1998. By then, he was having financial difficulties and suffering from depression, which had come on him the year before when he began to undergo odd experiences and sought help in a New Jersey psychiatric facility. Cullen later would file a formal complaint with the police against the doctor who took a blood sample upon his admission to the facility; he didn't like people sticking needles in him even though his own job was sticking needles in others.

In the end, Charles Cullen was at St. Barnabas for about four years as a regular full-time employee, but then for some reason he became a temporary employee on a per diem basis, a position from which he was ultimately fired in 1992. His colleagues didn't know why there was the shift in position, but obviously something was wrong. For the next eleven years, Cullen would bounce around to nine different jobs, and if something was wrong no one was talking about it or noting in on his employment record.

MOVING FROM HOSPITAL TO HOSPITAL

Charles Cullen continued to move from hospital to hospital in New Jersey, as well as engaging in bizarre behavior that apparently included further suicide attempts. In one attempt, he sealed his quarters to make them airtight, then piled coals in the bathtub and set them on fire. His goal was to choke to death by driving all the air out, much as one would with a gas oven, only in his case it didn't work.

Cullen left his job at St. Luke's, in Bethlehem, Pennsylvania, because they were looking into the seemingly abnormal deaths of some sixty-nine patients. Their investigation was fairly superficial, however, because a complete probe would have required exhuming all the bodies to detect any consistent irregularity, and the hospital ended the inquiry after only one body was exhumed. But the whole experience made Cullen nervous, and he quit and moved on to another position easily, because even though his record wasn't all that stellar nothing adverse had been noted on it.

To many people, this was the remarkable thing about Cullen, the ease with which he moved from one job to the next—he never had difficulty getting a new job. But, then, this may have been partly due to the shortage of nurses in the county or the difficulty in tracking nurses' employment records. Either way, Cullen sailed along smoothly for years until he was fired in October 2003 in connection with the death of Reverend Gall.

Somerset Medical Center told USA Today that when they checked Charles Cullen's background, all they could get from previous employers were the dates of his employment. What they subsequently learned horrified them when they realized he may have killed a dozen or more patients in the little more than a year he was on staff.

The harm to Somerset's professional reputation has been immense, and it could result in millions of dollars in damages being paid out for something they don't feel was their fault; namely, hiring Charles Cullen on the assumption that he was competent and trustworthy. How tragically wrong they were.

CULLEN'S INSTABILITY

The New York Times reported that Charles Cullen "attempted suicide at least three times, did four stints at mental hospitals, broke into a colleague's house . . . and was known in his neighborhood for his nighttime chasing of cats." Throughout his life, Cullen gave off warning signals that he should not be a caregiver, the Times observed, but all were ignored, to the fatal sorrow of many. They may be overstating the case a bit that he could be the worse serial killer in American history because, as we shall see, there are many people vying for that dubious distinction. Also, the Times's observation that "It was his guile, in part, that allowed him to elude capture all those years" may not be razor sharp since it was more a failure of institutional controls than anything else that allowed Cullen to slip in and out of jobs and quietly murder patients in their beds. Being professional, the Times followed its "guile" observation with much the same conclusion, saying that "Cullen was able to continue mostly because of systemic failures, and his career reveals gaping holes in hospital and government systems for weeding out people who harm patients."

In early 1992, Charles Cullen began working at Warren Hospital in Phillipsburg, New Jersey, and he realized he had found where he wanted to be. He was assigned to the graveyard shift, with few people around, and working in the intensive care unit. Filled with seriously ill patients, most of whom were unconscious and not expected to live, such units usually are supervised by only one nurse. Also, doctors almost never come around at that hour, powerful and therefore dangerous drugs are readily accessible, and a patient dying is not an unexpected event. To top it off, most nurses don't like working graveyard. So Cullen essentially was left in command of his own ship to do what he wanted, the perfect setting for a nurse who kills, In fact, in the past, a number of serial killers in the medical field have found working nights, with the sickest patients, to their liking.

While things "improved" at work, Charles Cullen's personal life was going to hell. His wife Adrienne filed for divorce in January 1993 and sought custody of their daughters. The grounds for separation were based on Cullen's odd behavior, such as refusing to talk to, touch, or sleep with her for several years, despite having sired two children. And he abused her dogs. The divorce went through and Cullen was left living in a small apartment for the next ten years. He ultimately became interested in a coworker, nurse Michelle Tomlinson, who did not return his favor. He nonetheless would moon around her at the hospital, making regular proposals, which she repeatedly rejected. Then, one morning just before sunrise, he smashed through the door of Tomlinson's residence and wandered through the place. She called the police and had him arrested. He, in turn, tried to commit suicide, which led to a two-month leave of absence, during which time he underwent counseling.

Then, on August 30, 1993, came an extraordinary event in this litany of already extraordinary events. Larry Dean was sitting with his mother, ninety-one-year-old Helen C. Dean, who was recovering from surgery for breast cancer. A male nurse not assigned to the ward entered Helen's room, told Larry to leave, and administered an injection no doctor had ordered. "He stuck me," she told her son when he returned. Relatives say Larry and Helen Dean complained to doctors and nurses, and even pointed out the nurse in question later, but no one took action.

The next day, Helen Dean was released from the hospital, even though "she looked green," according to her niece, Sharon Jones. That afternoon, Helen suffered heart failure and died. Larry Dean told the county prosecutor's office that his mother had been murdered. Tests were run on Helen looking for some one hundred different chemicals that might be present, but for some reason not for digoxin, which was later discovered to be Charles Cullen's poison of choice. So when nothing was found, the case was closed and Cullen continued doing what he did best.

Again, no entry was ever made on his record, no information released later to prospective employers. And again, he continued to endanger the community. Even though Charles Cullen's track record at Warren Hospital included at least two suicide attempts, a commitment to a psychiatric facility, and ouster from a job, a criminal conviction, and an allegation of murder, he stayed on the Warren payroll through 1993, and when people asked about this fact hospital personnel played dumb, as if they didn't know there might be a problem. When he eventually left Warren on his own at the end of the year, there was not way to check up on him.

MOVING ON WITH A CLEAN RECORD

From Warren Hospital, Charles Cullen went to Morristown Memorial, from where he was discharged for undisclosed reasons, as no one was offering any details. He moved next to Allentown Nursing Home, where, on May 8, 1998, he apparently administered an unauthorized shot of insulin to Francis Henry, another nurse's patient, which sent him into shock.

Months earlier, in October 1997, Cullen himself was admitted to Warren Hospital, then sent to Greystone psychiatric hospital. It was said that he had tried suicide once more. As many times as he attempted suicide, and with as much access as he had to dangerous drugs, some people wonder why he continually failed to die if, in fact, he seriously wanted to kill himself. But that is another issue.

Back on the street and sinking heavily into debt, on February 10, 1998, Charles Cullen was hired by Liberty Nursing and assigned to another difficult-to-staff ward, the "ventilature unit," where machines help patients breath. Meanwhile, the debate over who gave Francis Henry the shot of insulin dragged on, and his regular nurse, Kimberly Pepe, was fired. But Cullen was getting into more trouble on his own. In October 1998, two nurses saw him carrying syringes into the room of a patient not assigned to him. No one is sure what happened next, but the patient ended up with a broken arm and Cullen was fired. All this was kept from prospective employers who later contemplated hiring him as a nurse.

HOW THE TRACKING SYSTEM FAILS

Charles Cullen's story demonstrates the incredible ineptness of the medical licensing and monitoring system in protecting patients from predators. Employers are afraid to say anything of an uncomplimentary nature about former employees for fear of being sued for slander, and the government systems that should protect the public are wobbly and ineffective. It's open season on the patient, in other words, who is at the mercy of killers like Cullen.

Charles Cullen's case is probably not so extraordinary as the New York Times would have us believe. There have been a variety of stories just like his, such as the Glendale Adventist case, which happened at almost the same time. The system that processed Cullen processes everybody. Neither the Times nor you nor I nor anybody else has any idea as to how many predators are out there right now.

So what happened after Liberty fired Charles Cullen? He went looking for his sixth nursing job. Again, he was hired within a week, by Easton Hospital in Pennsylvania, and the next tragic scene was in the room of Ottomar Schramm, where his daughter, Kristin Toth, saw her father struggling to live with the help of an intravenous tube. As she and others watched, the male nurse on duty gave Mr. Schramm a shot. The next morning, Schramm was dead, and an autopsy later revealed lethal amounts of digoxin in his system.

The investigation of Ottomar Schramm's death was almost as curious as everything else surrounding the activities of Charles Cullen. Zachary Lysek, the Northampton County coroner, pursued Schramm's death for almost eight months. He always regarded it as murder, yet he never talked to Cullen even though Kristin Toth and the other nurses knew he administered the digoxin. Digoxin, incidentally, was listed as a cause of death. In spite of all this, Lysek never asked the district attorney's office to launch a criminal inquiry. And even though Ms. Toth told him about the mysterious man in her father's room, in the months since the death, he never learned Cullen's name.

Then, three years later, a colleague of Charles Cullen's called in a tip to Zachary Lysek fingering Cullen as the guilty one. Lysek called the police, but they couldn't establish a connection between Cullen and any of the deaths. Moreover, when Lysek contacted Easton Hospital, he was told there was no Charles Cullen on staff. This may have been true technically, because he was listed on a personnel agency's payroll instead.

Two days after New Year's 2000, however, a woman, Karin Ziemba, called the police because of the strong kerosene odor emanating from the apartment below hers, where her strange neighbor Charles Cullen lived. The police arrived to find another suicide in progress, with air vents sealed and charcoal burning in the bathtub, filling the place with carbon monoxide and driving all the oxygen out. They took Cullen to a medical center that specialized in emotional crises, but he was out on the street the next day and back working at Lehigh Valley. It was as if nothing out of the ordinary had happened.

THE END BEGINS AND OTHER NURSES ACT

The beginning of the end came in August 2002, and prophetically at the hands of Charles Cullen's coworkers at St. Luke's Hospital, who were highly agitated because their patients were in danger. They not only believed Cullen was a threat to those in their care, but also suspected that he may have been involved in the death of some of them. Bone-chillingly significant, they also believed that the hospital administration didn't want a messy investigation on their hands. The nurses expected St. Luke's would simply put a lid on the situation and allow Cullen to move on to do his evil elsewhere. So they called the police.

The trigger was finding discarded syringes and the drugs procainamide and nitroprusside on the ward where they weren't supposed to be. Everything pointed to Cullen. When the hospital administration questioned him, he refused to talk and quit a few days later, as was his pattern. After the police were called in, they in turn called in a medical investigator, who, in the end, came up with nothing.

Would the nurses' complaints have had any effect? The State Board of Nursing checked Cullen's record at St. Luke's, again only to come up with nothing. Of course, all efforts were focused on St. Luke's and not his record overall. But even if they had, there still was not enough evidence to go on, since anything of an unsubstantiated derogatory nature could lead to legal action on Cullen's part.

A short time later, Charles Cullen was working at Sacred Heart Hospital in Allentown, Pennsylvania, but that only lasted a little over two weeks because he didn't get along with the other nurses. In this never-never land of medicine, however, it didn't matter, and he returned to New Jersey where the shortage of nurses was still critical and as a result, credentials were not carefully checked. He soon landed a job at Somerset Medical Center in Somerville, where for the first time he ran afoul recordswise when the computer revealed he had been doing some things he shouldn't have, such as requisitioning medication for patients that were not his—Jin Kyung Han, for one. And the drugs he was requisitioning were not prescribed for these patients—Ms. Han had a heart attack due to the dioxin he administered to her.

An outside investigator was called in, who suggested that Han had been poisoned or given the wrong dose, but the hospital maintained that it was the herbal tea she drank. Again, no action was taken. Then, a few weeks later came the case of Florian Gall, who was not one of Cullen's patients even though Cullen hovered around the priest's room. Father Gall's sister , Lucille, remembers Cullen in particular. The computer would later show that Cullen had reviewed Gall's medical records on the night of June 27, and it was the next morning, June 28, that Gall died of a heart attack. The autopsy again revealed dioxin, which had never been prescribed for Gall, and Lucille Gall's outraged response was that "somebody killed him."

THE FINALE WAS APPROACHING

It wasn't over just yet for Charles Cullen, but it soon would be.

There was a lot of suspicions surrounding Cullen, and Somerset Medical Center decided to hire an outside investigator—but not to do anything about Cullen or to inform authorities about their suspicions. They just wanted it to go away. Then they made the mistake of consulting Dr. Steven Marcus, the head of New Jersey's poison control center, to see if he supported their herbal tea theory in the case of Jin Kyung Han. Marcus didn't, and he suggested it was a deliberate poisoning.

Things went from bad to worse for the hospital after that. First, Dr. Marcus and Somerset Medical began to argue and lose their respective tempers. Then Marcus threatened to report the hospital to state authorities. Finally, and worst of all, he had tape-recorded everything. Time to abandon ship!

Amidst all this probing, posturing, and covering up, another Somerset patient suffered a nonfatal insulin overdose on August 27. A few days later, yet another patient sustained a sharp drop in blood sugar and died less than an hour later. At this point, everybody was lining up to report anything and everything. What had been merely a computer glitch became a heavy-duty criminal investigation.

The odd part is, although computer records kept pointing to Charles Cullen, Somerset Medical let him continue working until October 31, at which point he was let go for lying on his job application. This delay may have allowed for the unnecessary death of several more patients. The investigators kept probing and finally arrested Cullen on December 12—five and a half months after he was accused of murdering Florian Gall.

What happened next shocked even the most hardened investigators.

THE CONFESSION

Once in police custody, Charles Cullen spilled out such a harrowing tale of his sixteen years as a caretaker-murderer that it could even make Hannibal Lecter's creator, Thomas Harris's blood run cold.

Cullen confessed to killing at least a dozen patients at Somerset Medical Center alone, and probably forty all told. The quiet, withdrawn demeanor of the slightly built, frail-looking Cullen was a sharp counterpoint to the horror he revealed to his transfixed interrogators. One couldn't be sure if he was quietly satisfied with the mercy he dispensed in killing or fiendishly proud of his omnipotent power over life itself. Either way, he admitted it openly and said he would not fight prosecution.

Charles Cullen was officially charged with the murder of Florian Gall and the attempted murder of the forty-year-old woman who suffered an insulin overdose. Although officials said that the investigation was just beginning and there was a lot more to look into, it was generally conceded that Cullen's case could become the most horrendous in New Jersey history. Ironically, it appeared that Cullen himself was trying to help by repeatedly pleading guilty before New Jersey Superior Court judge Paul Armstrong. Cullen was confused when Armstrong said he didn't want to accept a plea at that time since technically it was an arraignment hearing and not appropriate. He advised Cullen repeatedly to be silent and encouraged him to hire a lawyer or accept representation from a public defender. But Cullen clearly was relieved to have been finally caught and just wanted to get it over with as soon as possible. "I don't want to contest the charges," he said. " I plead guilty. I don't want to be represented. I don't intend to fight this."

In the end, bond was set at $1 million, Cullen accepted the services of a public defender, and he was transferred to a hospital for psychiatric evaluation. There, he awaits the next step of what many believe will be a very long trial.

There was one proviso to Charles Cullen's willingness to cooperate, however. He wasn't about to tell all unless the state of New Jersey agreed not to execute him. At that point, prosecutors hadn't announced what punishment they would be seeking, and Cullen's public defender, Johnnie Mask, said Cullen was "only charged with one murder and one attempted murder."

Death was okay for the victims of Charles Cullen, in other words, but not for Charles Cullen himself. As for a possible mercy killing defense, Dr. Michael Welner, an associate professor of psychiatry at New York University Medical Center and an expert on serial killers, said mercy killing is a common enough defense but a rationalization nonetheless that people turned to in an effort to convince themselves "they did the right thing."

REVIEWING AND ANALYZING KILLER CAREGIVERS

Officials are reviewing the death records at many of the nine previous hospitals where Charles Cullen was employed, and exhuming the bodies of patients he had contact with checking specifically for poisons. Naturally, they want to check all possible leads, including coworkers, who might be called as witnesses at the trial. In the community of Somerset, the general mood is one of shock and disbelief that such a killer could have thrived among them.

However, there is one thing about this case that experienced investigators are not eager to talk about: namely, this case may not be so easy to prove, suspicions and confessions not withstanding. Somerset County prosecutor Wayne Forrest said that while Cullen himself had supplied the names of some of his alleged victims, that still may not be enough or may even prove false, and fail to convince a judge or jury of his guilt.

For one thing, hospitals are easy places to commit murder without detection. Most patients are either very old or very young; they are sick, sometimes even comatose, and unable to communicate effectively. Death at a hospital is more common than rare, and, in fact, many patients are admitted with the strong possibility of dying there. "The killings are quiet," said James Thunder, a former prosecutor in Illinois, and the author of a number of works about detecting and preventing murder in medical facilities. "They are not obviously violent." Another expert, Dr. Michael Baden, New York City's former chief medical examiner, says, "These people tend to be serial killers. They tend to do it once or twice and see if they can get away with it. Apparently, for some people, it's a heady sensation to be able to kill someone quietly, without any fanfare." Baden also points out that in our cost-conscious world things have gotten more and more streamlined, and that means cutting corners not only at the grocery store and factory but at the hospital as well. It used to be that 60 percent of hospital deaths would merit an autopsy to establish the cause of death officially, but today insurance covers only about 10 percent of such cases, making the chance of detection even less.

Grotesquely, the reality is that hospitals are unwittingly in league with the murderer because they are leery of autopsies. That's because it might be discovered that the hospital made a mistake. And a mistake could mean a lawsuit. So it's easier to skip the autopsy, or, if a mistake is uncovered, fire somebody and keep the mistake secret.

GLENDALE AND OTHER PARALLEL CASES

Medical investigators assigned to the Charles Cullen case were reminded of a recent mercy killer at the Adventist Hospital in

Glendale, California. There, respiratory therapist Efren Saldivar was convicted of six murders and given the death penalty.

Saldivar's defense at first was that he was a compassionate "angel," but he finally admitted the motive was much more mundane and, therefore, even more reprehensible.

"We had too much work," he confessed. "When I was at my wits' end on the staffing, I'd look at the [patient] board. Who do we gotta get rid of?"

In another case, a nurse at a veterans' hospital in Massachusetts who was convicted of four murders in March 2001 admitted she reveled in the excitement of emergencies, so she would trigger them by giving patients overdoses of Adrenalin. In an unbelievable twist, she also employed these self-created emergencies to entice her boyfriend, who worked in the same hospital as an emergency medical technician. She even killed one patient so she could get off early and not be late for a date. So much for mercy.

Back at Somerset Medical Center, authorities, with the help of Dr. Baden, continue to check Charles Cullen's record. For example, they are checking deceased patients for drug overdoses and Cullen's access to the hospital pharmacy. Dennis Miller, the head of Somerset, said hospital pharmacists found an unusual number of orders connected to Cullen, leading them to suspect he had been poisoning patients. At the same time, Somerset launched a public relations campaign lauding its hundred-plus years of medical excellence and all the good and honorable professionals who work there. A good idea, no doubt, and inevitable, because as a community caregiver they couldn't afford to have their reputation ruined by a killer like Charles Cullen.

Hoping to learn more about serial killers, New Jersey police contacted Glendale murder detective Will Currie, who was lead investigator in the Saldivar case. Cullen and Saldivar are very similar. It took the Glendale police a year just to review hospital records, even utilizing the assistance of medical experts, and even longer to mount a case, which including identifying patients whose deaths were suspicious and exhuming bodies to test for poison. Twenty were tested and six found to be murdered, even though police were convinced Saldivar had killed many more. Quietly, New Jersey police hoped Charles Cullen would make it easier for them by naming names.

GLENDALE ADVENTIST HOSPITAL CASE

While the Cullen and Saldivar cases are very similar, one chief difference is that Saldivar romanticized himself as an "Angel of Death." One of his victims was Jean Coyle, who survived his injections and helped convict him in 1997, but who died at age sixty-five in December 2003 of respiratory distress. She was the only patient known to have survived Saldivar's ministrations, and her testimony helped convince him to plead guilty in 2002 to killing patients in 1996 and 1997.

Jean Coyle did have the satisfaction of attending the 2002 court hearing at which Efren Saldivar was sentenced to six life terms for the murders, and fifteen years to life for this attempt on her life.

2.

HOSPITAL KILLERS
AS A SERIOUS THREAT

There is a connection between hospital killers and those who try to bring them to justice. The case of Efren Saldivar, for example, the confessed Adventist Medical Center murderer, gave Joseph Deters the chills. It brought back the case of nurse's aide Donald Harvey in Ohio, who he helped convict in 1987 on twenty-four counts of aggravated murder. Harvey confessed to poisoning a number of seriously ill patients at Drake Memorial Hospital in the mid-1980s, who he rationalized were going to die soon anyway, and hastening the death of over fifty other critically ill men and women. He wanted to save them from pain, he said. He thought of it as an act of mercy. But Deters doesn't buy that morbidly romantic excuse. "Some killers use that to explain away horrific behavior," he said, speaking from his office in Ohio. "That's all bull crap. People who do this have a compulsion to kill."

Joseph Deters has reason to know because he was the Hamilton County assistant prosecutor when Harvey, then thirty-five, confessed to murder. Harvey used rat poison, cyanide, arsenic, and cleaning fluid to kill patients under his care. Deters saw him convicted and sentenced to three consecutive life terms.

The lineup of so-called mercy killers is a lot more crowded than people realize, and for all their surprise they don't consider that these are only the one who have been caught.

Robert Diaz, a nurse a Community Hospital of the Valley in Perris, California, injected a dozen older patients with a poisonous drug. He was caught in 1981 and sentenced to death in 1984. Diaz hadn't murdered at just one hospital but at a number of them. Sounds a lot like Charles Cullen.

And it's not just nurses who kill. Michael Swango, an Illinois physician, was caught and imprisoned in New York after a string of sudden deaths at hospitals across the country was finally connected to him.

One of the terrifying things about many of these cases is how hard it is to nail the killer, how many times the killer slips away. Dozens of times, Charles Cullen could have or should have been caught, but each time a lie, a mistake let him slip away. Police arrested Efren Saldivar in March 1998, holding him in jail for three days, during which time he revealed in a taped confession that between 1989 and 1997 he killed terminally ill Glendale Adventist patients by suffocating them or injecting them with drugs. But after being detained from March 11 to 13, Saldivar was released because investigators had no other evidence that he actually committed the crimes. The next day, the hospital fired him along with forty-five of his coworkers. He dropped out of sight, secluding himself at home, while the police attempted to build a case against him. He finally appeared on 20/20 and recanted his confession. This type of thing makes it hard to build a case that will hold up in court, especially since Saldivar had told police he got the idea for overdosing patients from news reports about a health care worker in Chicago who killed patients.

Murderous nurses and doctors, naturally, jar those hospital personnel who are dedicated healers devoted to their patients and their calling. The very idea of killers loose in hospitals has prompted much soul-searching among the members of the American Hospital Association, an organization representing some five thousand facilities nationwide. Spokesman Rich Wade says, "Our members are wondering how you can spot something like this through background checks and reference checks before it becomes a problem."

Wade goes on to note that such killers are extremely rare, and that all hospitals have stringent security measure in place to safeguard patients. Dangerous drugs are kept under lock and key, and there are elaborate tracking systems to prevent theft. Beyond that, personnel are required to report any suspicious behavior on the part of colleagues. Still, he also admits it can be hard to determine if a worker is hastening the death of a critically ill patient because death is not always unexpected.

Glendale Adventist Hospital defended its drug storage policies, even though they had been cited by the Los Angeles County Department of Health and Human Services for failure to maintain tougher security procedures. Despite their arguments, clearly Efren Saldivar was able to access them rather easily.

Glendale Police sergeant Rick Young has called the Saldivar case very difficult to prove. That's because it would involve exhuming bodies to see if poisonous drugs were present. The same could be true for the Cullen case, and it may proceed as slowly as Saldivar's did.

Over a year after Efren Saldivar made his confession, the baffling Angel of Death case was still open with no arrest. Saldivar was fired from his job and his nursing license was suspended, but he was free while a task force of six police officers tried to figure out what had happened. It was Glendale's most extensive homicide investigation ever, searching for victims to prove a crime even had occurred. This same type of bottleneck threatens the Cullen investigation and could lead to delays and an eventually unprovable case. Glendale evidence was buried somewhere in one of several area cemeteries, and once located the cooperation of relatives is needed in order to exhume the body for examination. But some of the Glendale bodies might have been cremated, or shipped away for burial. Also, the disturbance of their loved ones final resting place may prove objectionable for some families. Careful not to divulge any of their tactics, police have been close-mouthed about the number of bodies they have investigated and where and when they were exhumed. Naturally, all of this is disturbing to the families involved.

Under questioning, Efren Saldivar told police the criteria he employed in deciding whether to perform a mercy killing. The patient had to be unconscious. The patient had to have a "do not resuscitate" order indicated on his or her chart. And the patient had to "look like they [sic] were ready to die." When the case first broke, Los Angeles authorities formed a task force to handle the investigation. It promised to be as involved as the Cullen case would become. For example, a year after Saldivar's confession authorities still hadn't contacted family members because they weren't certain who were really victims, and they estimated it could involve exhuming some five hundred bodies first to find out.

It all started with an anonymous phone call to Glendale police on March 3, 1998. The caller said Efren Saldivar, a respiratory therapist, "help a patient die fast" on or about February 16, 1998. The police immediately followed up on the tip and on March 11 Saldivar came to the station as requested. He was there several days, during which time he admitted killing a patient at Glendale Adventist about six months after he started working there in 1989. He said the patient had been taken off life support but wasn't dying, so he cut off his oxygen supply. Saldivar's explanation was that it upset him to see a terminally ill patient being kept alive and in pain and he helped the patient die easily. He said he had first been inspired to do it by a TV news magazine story, and then starting in 1992 he began killing more patients with injections of morphine, Pavulon, and succinylcholine chloride, the later two drugs paralyzing the muscles and therefore suffocating the patient.

Appearing on 20/20 in April 1998, Efren Saldivar changed his story and said he never killed anyone. He made it all up, he said, because he wanted to die but couldn't bring himself to commit suicide so he thought he'd let the state do it for him. Ultimately, he did get so far as prison. His story, meanwhile, generated a deluge of phone calls to the hospital and some 258 meetings with family members about what might have really happened to their relatives. At the same time, not only were police checking hundreds of medical files, they were checking other mercy killing cases around the country. They also engaged the services of Michael Baden, forensic sciences director for the New York state police, who specializes in notorious murder cases, including those of John Kennedy and Martin Luther King, and a case very much like the Glendale one, Long Island serial killer Richard Angelo. Angelo, a nurse at Good Samaritan Hospital, was sentenced to sixty-one years to life for killing four patients after thirty-three bodies were exhumed and traces of Pavulon were found in six of them.

Glendale police weighed Saldivar's confession against the actual evidence. They searched for drugs in the bodies and then determined whether as patients they had been prescribed those drugs. But with over five hundred deaths at Glendale Adventist every year normally, and with most of them involving the sick and elderly, it wasn't an easy task.

Sadly, cases like those of Efren Saldivar and Charles Cullen are only the most recent over the years. A similarly sensation case in New Jersey involved Dr. Carl Coppolino, an anesthesiologist, who killed his wife, Dr. Carmela Coppolino, in 1965. The initial cause of death was challenged by her father, and the exhumed body revealed concentrations of succinylcholine chloride. Then there was the case of vocational nurse Genene Jones of Kerrville, Texas, who was convicted of killing a fifteen-month-old child with an injection of the same drug. In all these cases, investigators need proof. And the problem with proof is that it is close to impossible to exhume the bodies of all the victims because they are buried in the many places these nurses worked. Police were forced into a game of Russian roulette, hoping the bodies they exhume are the right ones, that traces of poison will be found. They don't want to exhume bodies only to needlessly inflict emotional pain on families.

3.

THE ROLE OF NURSES
IN ACTION

A question that keeps coming up in many people's minds throughout the Cullen horror is, What about the other nurses? What were they all doing? Were they blind to what was going on? Or were they incompetent or just plain stupid?

As noted earlier, some did try to thwart Charles Cullen. In fact, for over a year before Cullen's arrest nurses at St. Luke's Hospital were suspicious of him and concerned he might be killing patients, and they filed a report with both the state nursing board and the police. And when he was finally fired in June 2002, they alerted his next employer that he might be a danger. He was escorted out of St. Luke's by security guards because nurses believed he was stockpiling dangerous drugs he wasn't supposed to have. And when the cardiac care nurses were suspicious that someone was causing the excessive number of life-threatening "code blue" emergencies in their unit,

Cullen was who they focused on. They did what they could by alerting others, a lot more than anyone else, including St. Luke's management and state authorities, did at the time. And they prodded people at places such as Easton Hospital, where Cullen had worked in 1998, to investigate a mysterious death that had occurred while he was there.

Nurses at Liberty Nursing and Rehab Center and Sacred Heart Hospital, both in Allentown, pressured their respective administrations to fire Cullen after he had been working at either place for less than a month. So the buzz in the nursing community was that Charles Cullen was serious trouble.

Yet, despite the buzz, Cullen moved on to two more hospitals, where no negative notations were made in his file and no one alerted authorities of anything suspicious. He walked into these jobs just like he had the others, with a clean record. No one wanted to risk being sued.

Admittedly, nurses did not suspect Charles Cullen every place he worked. He may have seemed a touch odd but not dangerous. Initially polite and helpful, he was later recalled by some for his apparent idiosyncrasies, such as avoiding eye contact, almost never sitting down, and never eating at work. Looking back, they did recall a greater number of code blues when he came on staff; in fact, some said the number doubled. Yet a hospital spokesperson disputes this, saying the increase can be attributed to increasing numbers of trauma patients being admitted to the hospital.

Oddly, when there was a code blue Cullen would carefully remove any trash from the room, as if there might be an empty medicine vial in it that he didn't want anybody to find. In retrospect, this was probably exactly what he was doing, nurses now think.

As Susan Bartos, a now retired nurse who worked alongside Cullen at St. Luke's, told one reporter, "You'd take such good care of your patients and see a light at the end of the tunnel. Then he'd come on, and their heart rate and blood pressure would rise. But you couldn't prove anything."

Some nurses believe that Charles Cullen put drug overdoses in drip bags, which feed drugs through a tube into the patient's arm. That's what Efren Saldivar did at Glendale Adventist. Some nurses felt something was not right with their patients simply because the drastic changes they underwent rarely happened that suddenly. For a patient recovering nicely at dinnertime to die at midnight was most unusual, but that's what happened when Cullen was around.

When Cullen was fired from St. Luke's, several nurses checked their records to see if he was on duty when their patients died, and were sickened to learn how often he was. While that coincidence didn't prove anything, it triggered enough suspicion that the nurses notified the hospital manager, the Pennsylvania State Board of Nursing, the police, the county coroners, and Cullen's next employer, Sacred Heart Hospital in Allentown. The nurses were determined that nobody else be killed. Bartos summarized other nurses' evaluation of Cullen: "They said he'd come on and people would die."

While the nursing board didn't act at first, coroners in the two counties where facilities were located, Northampton County's Zachary Lysek and Lehigh County's Scott Grim, had heard enough to launch an investigation. Lysek was already troubled by the death of seventy-eight-year-old Ottomar Schramm at Easton Hospital back in 1998, and now he had the name of the possible perpetrator to pin it on. Ironically, Cullen wasn't charged with Schramm's death until

December 18, 2003, after being charged with murder and attempted murder in New Jersey on the fifteenth.

Questions about Charles Cullen forced him out of St. Luke's, but he was hired by Sacred Heart a month later. It wasn't going to be like before, however, and this time the nurses' informal network was tracking him, and Sacred Heart staff were getting warning phone calls from colleagues at St. Luke's. And then there was Kimberly Pepe, a nurse at Sacred Heart who had previously worked at Liberty Nursing, where she had been fired when one of her patients died. She was convinced that Cullen had killed the patient, and she was suing Liberty and naming him in the suit. She and other nurses also warned Sacred Heart about Cullen and threatened to quit. A few days later, he was gone.

Sacred Heart's chief executive officer Jim Seitzinger, however, was very pragmatic about the whole thing. He told one reporter that he didn't ask, and didn't want to know, why everyone was against Charles Cullen. "Everyone is afraid of being sued," he said.

And nobody wanted to get involved in a mess. So instead of trying to get Cullen off the streets, people just wanted him to move on and get out of their lives. They wanted to avoid hassle, and they were nervous about the legal implications. And while the nurses did take action, it was mostly to get him out of the hospital and not to put him in jail.

Many nurses who dealt with Charles Cullen understood that while some did what they could about him, suspicion alone doesn't always correct things. The problem is finding proof that will stand up in court. As Susan Bartos saw it, "Without toxicology, how do you know? People do get sick and have heart rates of 150. . . . No families pushed it, so what do you say? Let's exhume a body? Then you are opening yourself up to lawsuits."

The New York Times summed up with the final irony. "His nursing licenses were in order. He was, in theory, ready to be hired somewhere." That's not quite true. By that time, all the nurses' complaints would have kept Charles Cullen from being hired or staying hired for more than a few days. It was over for Cullen and his fellow nurses made sure of it.

4.

SERIAL KILLING IS NOT UNUSUAL AND MOSTLY AMERICAN

The most unusual thing about the Cullen case is that it is not unusual.

Charles Cullen is a type of serial killer, and we have had many types of serial killers throughout history and all around the world. A serial killer is someone who kills a number of individual people over time, as opposed to a mass murderer who kills a number of people all at one time. FBI profilers further define a serial killer as one who kills with a cooling-off period after each killing, and who kills for no apparent reason—at least, not apparent to the police or others searching for the killer.

Many serial killers kill for reasons that are often hinged upon either a mental disorder, a sexual disorder, feelings of self-loathing, or a need for revenge. This group includes the likes of Ted Bundy, Charles Manson, Edward Gein, John Wayne Gacy, Jeffrey Dahmer,

Gary Gilmore, and David Berkowitz. Manson, for example, wanted to start a race war where many would be killed and he would emerge as king. And Berkowitz, a paranoid schizophrenic, claimed membership in a satanic cult called the "Four P Movement," based in California, that was a spin-off of the "Process Church of Final Judgment," somehow connected to Manson as well as the Church of Scientology. What is surprising to many about the Cullen case is that the killer was a caregiver, one supposedly devoted to nurturing. His victims were being put out of their pain and misery, according to him, so the motive was supposedly mercy.

Another type of serial killer is the "bad seed" born with a killer instinct and driven to kill. William Archerd was such a bad seed who loved medicine, wanted to be a doctor but couldn't afford medical school, and instead in 1940 became an attendant at Camarillo State Hospital in California, where he was trained in administering insulin shock treatment for relief from symptoms of mental illness. Ten year later, he was arrested for the illegal use of morphine and sent to jail for three years. When he got out, he continued trafficking in drugs, including insulin, and was arrested for murdering his fourth wife with it (he had seven wives altogether, three of whom died under suspicious circumstances). In 1968, he was convicted of murder and sentenced to death but like Manson, was spared when California banned capital punishment.

One of the most common explanations for why serial killers kill is abuse and personality-twisting experiences early in life. Most psychologists agree that childhood impacts adulthood, and a key part of childhood is the bonding between parent and child. Without it, we are told, the adult is incapable of love, sympathy, or regret. He or she engages in antisocial behavior or become a sociopath who preys on others. Too, many things the parents does or does not do are linked to such behavior, such as malnutrition during pregnancy, alcoholism, drug addiction, child abandonment, and physical abuse, all of which can produce children with damaged brains and warped personalities.

To illustrate, the FBI studied the lives of thirty-six killers for three years and concluded that they all shared several common deficits from childhood; namely, physical or sexual abuse and negative role models. In most cases, the abuse was deliberate. Experts conclude, therefore, that the evolution of the serial killer is more often intentional than accidental.

A curious aspect of serial killing is geography. Except for Antarctica, there have been cases of serial killers everywhere in the world. However, most are American. With only 5 percent of the world's population, the United States has 75 percent of the world's reported serial killers, 85 percent of them since 1980.

Europe follows the U.S. with 16 percent—Great Britain with 28 percent of that total, Germany with 27 percent, and France with 13 percent. Most serial killings in the United States seem to be in California, Florida, New York, Texas, and Illinois. Experts believe this is normal, since those states have the greatest population concentrations. Charles Cullen was in Pennsylvania and New Jersey, two heavily populated states.

One characteristic common to many serial killers is a hypnotic attraction for the opposite sex. Charles Manson's family members continue to adore him. Squeaky Fromm, for instance, while serving time in a West Virginia prison, learned that Manson might be paroled in California. She escaped from prison, and began walking west so she could be with him. Also, when these killers are brought to trial, the courtroom often is filled with admiring women who want to care for them, even marry them. Charles Schmid, for example, on trial in Arizona as the "Pied Pier of Tucson," had a cheering section of teenaged girls, and Ted Bundy had an active group of young women with long brown hair parted in the middle just like his victims who wrote him love letters in prison. Bundy eventually married one of them and fathered a child by artificial insemination before he was executed in 1989. The lover of "Hillside Strangler" Kenneth Bianchi tried to murder someone while he was in jail in order to shift blame away from Bianchi and set him free. And Richard Ramirez, the "Night Stalker," a devil worshipper, had his own fan club when he was on trial for thirteen murders.

Serial murder dates back to ancient times, and probably before recorded history. We know, for example, that the Roman Locusta was a notorious serial poisoner a few years after the birth of Christ, the Yemini Zu Xhdnatir used to toss young boys to their death after violating them sexually, and the Iranian assassins cult believed murder was a tribute to their god, which they pursued well into the nineteenth century and later by strangling people with scarves they wore around the waist.

In Europe, serial killers included the Frenchman Gille de Rais, the richest man in France in the thirteenth century, who killed a hundred some children in sex rituals, or English cook Margaret Davey, who poisoned a string of employers. Ironically, she was boiled alive in 1542. In the seventeenth century, Hungarian countess Erzebet Bathory tortured invalids and the sick because she found it amusing. The only difference among all these killers is how their victims died.

In America, predators preyed upon travelers along wilderness trails, such as the Natchez Trace north of New Orleans along the Mississippi River. Herman Mudgett entrapped young women visitors to the 1893 Chicago World's Fair in an elaborate home that he called his "murder castle" and killed at least twenty-seven of them. In the 1880s, New England nurse Jane Toppan began poisoning some of her patients, ultimately killing between thirty-one and a hundred.

Serial killing thrives in America to this day, and while in the first half of the century major cases surfaced maybe twice a year, nowadays it three per month.

MEDICAL MURDERS

To the surprise of most people, there seems to be more serial killers in the field of medicine that one would imagine for such a profession. One obvious advantage is that patients are accessible, trusting, and mostly defenseless to fend off a killer. In fact, the victim's ignorance of medicine usually makes him or her cooperative, doing whatever he is told with complete faith that it is the right thing. Doctors, nurses, attendants—all are supposedly dedicated to the patient's well-being. Plus, as mentioned earlier, death in a hospital is not unexpected, so the chance of detection is relatively slight, which is why some people have been able to kill for years. In fact, discovery usually comes only when there are too many deaths or when a coworker questions a blatantly improper procedure.

But one of the most puzzling questions in a case like Charles

Cullen's is "why." Perhaps it's because he can relive it forever as the all-consuming experience of his life.

One of the most common types of medical murders is the mercy killing, a misnomer since the actual act can be painful and even sadistic. Another type is the "hero," where the killer appears to be trying to save the victim's life and for which effort he or she is praised. The victim is always on the brink of being saved, but, at the last minute, efforts fail. Baby killer Genene Jones was this type of killer, along with Richard Angelo.

Then, astonishingly, there is the murder-for-profit killer. Dr. Morris Bolber in Philadelphia and Amy Archer-Gilligan in Connecticut started their clinics with the intention of killing patients, and Missouri dentist Glennon Engelman was a profit-seeking murderer.

5.

THE WHY OF SERIAL MURDERS

We are always stunned by the story of the serial killer and we're not quite sure why. For one thing, the questions of motive and methodology always haunts us. Why murder? Why this particular victim? Why would someone become a serial killer in the first place? Most experts agree that there are a number of reasons for anything so antisocial, so inhuman, so perverse as serial killing. As with many complicated relationships, there is no one answer, but there are several reasons that help explain the phenomenon somewhat. The FBI groups these killers in three broad categories: the criminal, the sexual, and the personal.

The criminal category involves profit, regardless of the method, be it robbery, kidnapping, murder for hire. The sexual involves gratification of need, be it symbolic or even bizarre, such as mutilation or cannibalism. The personal involves a relationship, even one between two people who technically don't know each other.

With the criminal, we find thieves, extortionists, and gangsters.

With the sexual, we find such killers as Edmund Kemper, the "Coed Killer," who'd pick up hitchhikers in the Fresno area, where he lived, murder them, bring them home to a house he shared with his shrewish mother, have sex with various body parts, then bury the bodies in the woods after decapitating them first and leaving their heads by the roadside. He also killed his grandparents, then his mother, whom he had sex with after she was dead and then kept her head in the kitchen to use as a dartboard. Ironically, he frequented a neighborhood bar popular with police and his many police friends innocently kept him apprised of their progress in trying to solve the case. With the personal category, however, we have mercy killing and hero homicide. The FBI describes the mercy killer as having a warped desire to end suffering by killing the sufferer, and the hero as creating a life-or-death situation into which he or she can intervene and almost save the day.

IS IT MERCY KILLING?

Nurses, multiple killing linked in troubling trend: Mercy not seen as the motivation.

> *—Joyce Howard Price, Washington Post, December 7, 1998*

Cloaked in supposed kindness, the phrase "mercy killing" rolls off the tongue with amazing ease. But where's the mercy? Take the case of Kristen Gilbert, the former nurse at a veterans' hospital in Northampton, who allegedly killed three patients and tried to kill two others. Charged with murder, she claims she was acting out of the goodness of her heart, that she deserved understanding and maybe even gratitude for saving people from needless suffering.

Or take the case of Orville Majors, a nurse from Clinton, Indiana, who was charged with killing eight patients following an investigation into some 166 suspicious deaths in Clinton. He, too, claimed mercy as a motive.

Since 1974, when a Scottish nurse was convicted of killing a patient with an insulin injection, at least nineteen nurses have been charged with murdering patients, according to Beatrice Crofts Yorker, a lawyer and professor of nursing at San Francisco State University who has been tracking the trend since 1986. So what is it that turns a caregiver into a murderer? "The classic cases are those who believe they are ending the suffering of very, very ill patients," says Rick Wade, speaking for the American Hospital Association. It's out of a sense of compassion, to stop a patient's suffering, that they kill. "Bull," says Joseph Deters, who as a prosecuting attorney in Ohio convicted Donald Harvey of killing thirty-seven patients. Mercy killing is just an excuse, according to Deters, a gimmick.

But Beatrice Yorker has a more professional medical explanation: these killers are sociopaths obsessed with feeling important, heroic, needed. They often surround themselves with symbols of success and power to prove their own worth—be it financial, political clout, or just plain pomp and circumstance. They take advantage of others to prove how important they themselves are. For the killer nurse, it's the absolute power of life and death they have over patients. They are "particularly drawn to the health care field because it offers them a vulnerable population," Yorker says. More troubling, such aberrant behavior, no doubt evident outside the hospital setting as well, does not show up on hospital records. For example, Charles Cullen's suicide attempts, or his strange behavior in the Navy, where he was found steering a submarine while wearing nurse's garb.

As so often is the case, the system would seem to protect the killer nurse and not the public. Hospitals could "get into problems with the Americans With Disabilities Act," says Michelle Slattery of the American Nurses Association, if they refuse to hire a qualified nurse with a history of mental problems.

Beatrice Yorker reports that the number of killer nurses around the country is very small. "There are 2.6 million registered nurses in the United States," she says. "Unfortunately, when something like this happens it erodes public trust in the nursing profession."

Two findings in Yorker's studies are not fully explained yet disturbing nonetheless. First, the victims are not always sick. She cites cases involving killing otherwise healthy children who came to the doctor's office for immunization, or killing healthy women who came to the hospital for a cancer screening. In an outrageous example from Kristen Gilbert's case, Gilbert asked her boss if she could go home early if one of their patients, Kenneth Cutting, died. Innocently unthinking, the supervisor said "yes" and Gilbert murdered Cutting. As a final touch, she telephoned his wife at home to tell her that her husband was dead. The second finding is that these murders are being committed independently all over the country with some regularity and are not just coincidental. "The majority of the perpetrators are reenacting some kind of trauma on someone less powerful than they are," Yorker concludes.

6.

ARE LAWYERS TO BLAME?

We are a litigious society, quick to drag someone into court the minute we feel wronged or, worse, we smell money, and lawyers are quick to accommodate that need. What to some is justified redress to others is wanton greed. And while it is good to have a means to recourse, often the awards seem ludicrous, as in such cases as the "Stella award,: named for eighty-one-year-old Stella Liebeck who won a $2.9 million judgment against McDonald's for spilling a cup of scalding hot coffee on herself. After the case of Charles Cullen became public, an advertisement appeared that seemed to be trolling for potential clients.

The ad was sponsored by InjuryBoard.com, a personal injury website, and provided a complete summary of the Cullen case, with specific reference to Cullen's confessions that he had "'mercy killed' 30 to 40 patients since 1987" and "killed dozens of 'very sick' patients to alleviate their pain and suffering." It goes on to inform readers that he has already "pled guilty to all charges," and that he did not "plan to fight this."

With the door wide open, InjuryBoard.com offered the sound advice that those who believed they might have a case against Cullen or any of the hospitals that employed him needed to act fast and contact an attorney to help protect their "legal rights."

InjuryBoard.com is not a law firm, and while it claims that it isn't a lawyer referral service either, users are only one click away from a sponsoring firm while visiting its website. Sponsoring firms financially support the site's operation and do not collect fees from potential clients unless they recover money. According to the "About" feature of their web site:

InjuryBoard.com provides the general public with easily accessible legal and medical material in an effort to help consumers better understand any injury or medical condition that has negatively impacted their lives.

Is this ambulance chasing, or is it a community service? The families whose deceased loved ones were entrusted with Charles Cullen and his employers will certainly cling to their personal perspectives on this. After all, they've not only suffered a loss, but they're now being forced to relive an experience that they thought had been put to rest, and it's quite possible that many of them feel that the violation they're currently enduring requires monetary compensation. If it is their opinion that a breakdown in the system caused their pain, a system that on a good day sees a profit for itself, then it is easy to argue that compensation is just.

Of course, Charles Cullen was not responsible for every patient that died while he was employed as a caregiver, yet through this aggressive pursuit of legal reparation, every family that came in contact with Cullen is left wondering if something was taken from them. In the end, whether the cause of death was truly natural, or Charles Cullen's lethal syringe, something was taken from all of these families—the security of knowing that their loved one died peacefully, "when it was their time." What's left for them is a lingering doubt, that there could have been more time to be had, and a devastating "what if," what if their choice to utilize one care provider over another had deadly consequences. To have this experience intentionally thrust upon those who in fact did not suffer directly as a result of Cullen's actions, so that others— families and lawyers—might receive a cash reward is beyond unfortunate, it's cruel.

The right to know will always come at the expense of the shelter not knowing provides. Regardless of the moral dilemma this creates, there's also a balance to it—after all, those families not directly linked to Cullen's actions may have originally been in the minds of those who chose not to sound the alarms without evidence. Unfortunately, when there's money involved there's always the potential to throw the most balanced system off, and like moths to a flame, the mentality that inspired sites like InjuryBoard.com will inevitably draw out those looking to profit off the system by whatever means necessary. "Can I sue?" becomes the question, and if there's money to be made, then there's someone out there to say "Yes, you can, and I'll be happy to represent you for a percentage." This could be the dialogue exchange that scares hospital administrators most, enough to convince them to let a clearly disturbed man loose on their colleagues and the world. To let someone else handle it and brave the firing squad of scandal and potential lawsuits, is as realistic a motivation as is the desire to keep something quiet out of respect for those who need not be distressed by it.

Ultimately, there is no one answer, no one specific cause that allows predators like Cullen to thrive for as long as they do, but there are a lot of independent factors that come into play. Aggressive litigation is as much a part of the problem as it is a means to rectify, and while it is for each individual to decide its place in their lives, it cannot be denied as a fixed piece in how our modern society functions. It's not going anywhere, and the only way to counter its abuse is for good people to stand up and do the right thing. In the case of Charles Cullen, there were some who tried to, but it wasn't enough, and people died as a result—right, wrong, or reward won't change that.

7.

IS A WEAK NURSE TRACKING SYSTEM TO BLAME?

Charles Cullen was able to keep his license, even after being fired from several jobs, because hospitals, state regulators, and prosecutors didn't share information. He later confessed he had given lethal injections to thirty to forty critically ill patients during his sixteen-year career in Pennsylvania and New Jersey. His modus operandi was to administer a heart medication that was readily available to him in the hospitals where he worked. While Cullen's psychological state was a mix of various motives, an inclination toward suicide, and the belief that he was doing good, he claims the murders were all mercy killings.

Reporting a problem doesn't necessarily mean that anything will be done about it. The Liberty Nursing and Rehabilitation Center in Allentown, which fired Cullen for given patients injections they were not supposed to have, notified the State Health Department about him but not the nursing board, which could have revoked his license. Instead, he just continued on his lethal way. And while St Luke's Hospital reported him to the nursing board, they refused to inform his next employer. They didn't want to violate Cullen's "right to privacy."

Several things make the identification and apprehension of murdering caregivers difficult in our medical system. Breakdowns in communication among hospitals, local and state regulators, professional organizations, and others is a major problem, and millions of dollars have been spent trying to remedy the situation. But too often it's people who get in the way. As Dennis Miller, the head of Somerville Medical, says, technology didn't fail them; it was the human factors that let Cullen go undetected and unpunished for so long.

One of these factors is the severe shortage of nurses. Because of understaffing, shortcuts are taken and problems overlooked. Nurses like Charles Cullen are hired without much in the way of background checks or too many questions asked. Also, sometimes quirks in behavior are tolerated just to keep staffing quotas filled.

Charles Cullen pled guilty to attempted murder on June 15 and murder on June 28. But when Paul Armstrong, the judge, set aside the guilty pleas pending further investigation, it left the medical community around the country and the world stunned. (Ironically, Armstrong presided over another landmark hearing in the 1970s, the right-to-die case of Karen Ann Quinlin.) Robert Conroy, the attorney for the Medical Society of New Jersey, summed up the case this way: "Unfortunately, you have bureaucrats regulating nurses in the hospital setting and it's easier to just let some [nurses] resign, retire, or move on to the next job rather than to conduct an investigation and take disciplinary action—all of which could result in an unlawful termination lawsuit." Given the circumstances, he thinks some nurse-starved hospitals may be "willing to look aside, hold their breath, and pray for luck."

Warning signals are ignored in light of the need for nurses. The desire to get rid of a problem nurse as quickly and cleanly as possible by pushing him or her on to another hospital for someone else to worry about is common. Severance with no fuss, no muss is what is wanted. No complaints on the departing nurse's record means no messy lawsuits. Yet anybody familiar with Charles Cullen's record would have been more than apprehensive about hiring him.

Another oddity: While a nurse's record may be thin at the local and state levels, the National Practitioner Data Bank and the Healthcare Integrity and Protection Date Bank, created in 1990 to collect information about doctors, dentists, and nurses, is virtually unknown in the medical world and therefore not accessed with any regularity. The two banks have very different intentions, says Mark Pincus, acting director of data banks for the Health Resources and Services Administration. The practitioner bank serves as a repository for all medical licensing and privileged information data, as well as any actions taken by professional societies, Medicare, and Medicaid against doctors and dentists. Accessible to hospital, managed care, and other health care organization, the healthcare integrity bank was originally intended to detect Medicare cheats, and other government agencies and health plans can utilize it to see what they have to say about a given health professional.

Beatrice Yorker, researching murders in hospitals for the past sixteen years, believes she has proven there have been at least forty-two medical serial killers, and is still investigating another possible twenty-five, who all together are responsible for over five hundred murders. Two of the killers are doctors, the rest nurses. Her most recent murderer, Dr. Michael Swango, was sentenced to life in 2000. Yorker feels a lot more needs to be done to identify these murderers, especially the nurses. "Hospital risk management needs to focus more on patient safety," she says, "and focus less on disgruntled nurses who were denied employment. There needs to be a database for unsafe nurses."

8.

THE FLYING LAWSUITS

Charles Cullen and other nurses who kill unleash swarms of lawsuits flying off in all directions. By March 15, 2004, investigators were still putting together the enormous jigsaw puzzle of erratic behavior and murder that was Cullen's life, but that didn't keep lawyers from filing so many petitions that it seemed like everybody was suing everybody else. Obviously, they all targeted Cullen. Any of his proven victims' families probably have grounds to sue him, the key word being "proven." He claims he killed up to forty people, but which people? And even if their heirs win in court, where does the money come from? Certainly not from Cullen, since he no doubt is broke. When people sue, they usually are looking for deep pockets.

And then there's the question of who else besides Cullen could be sued. The stockholders in the hospital, the hospital directors and administrators, the hospital's personnel department, employees in that department who were supposed to have checked Cullen's references, the insurance company, other nurses and doctors who should have spotted Cullen as trouble? How about the hospitals up the line suing each other in turn for not passing on the word that Cullen was trouble?

Confusing, yes, but that never stopped an aggressive lawyer or a determined client. It certainly hasn't stopped the victims' relatives. And it hasn't stopped equally aggressive and determined insurance companies from trying to avoid paying out any settlements. It looks to be a long, hard battle for all sides involved.

Included in the first wave of cases are three suits brought by the families of people Charles Cullen killed in Pennsylvania. They are claiming that the hospitals hired Cullen without properly checking his background, that they didn't supervise him adequately, and that they engaged in a conspiracy of silence by not alerting his subsequent employers about him. Plus, the corporation that used to own Easton Hospital has also filed a lawsuit. They are charging that the nursing employment agency that handled Cullen is liable for damages.

In the end, a lot of people are going to spend a lot of money, lose a lot of money, maybe lose their jobs or go out of business, generally end up poorer and hating Charles Cullen even more. The only thing that's for certain is that more legal action is on the way.

For example, a New Jersey attorney says he is thinking of litigating on behalf of three families of onetime patients at Somerset Medical Center, the theory being that anybody in any hospital where Cullen worked could have been a victim. And Cullen, for his part, will be forced into the tough position of having to prove he didn't kill somebody. The common threat is that even without much evidence, why not give it a shot?

And the lawsuits aren't just limited to the deceased. Luis Ramos of Allentown is suing St. Luke's because of complications following a gastric bypass in 2002 that left him disabled. He had briefly stopped breathing, lost control of his kidneys, and been unconscious for a week. The family suspects he was poisoned, and his wife remembers the nurse whose picture she later saw on television as being the same one who was hanging around her husband's room. Responding to the Ramoses' claims, frustrated hospital officials say their only defense is to reiterate that Charles Cullen has only been charged with the murder of a priest and the attempted murder of a woman.

Reaching further, the widower of forty-one-year-old Debra Shachter, who underwent brain surgery at St. Luke's, is suing. A spokesperson for the hospital has said that Charles Cullen didn't work in that part of the hospital and therefore couldn't have been involved in her death, which is clearly explained in her medical records. "St. Luke's is increasing appalled by the manner in which surviving family members of patients who have died in area hospitals have been exploited—either by attorneys or by the media," the spokesperson said in a statement. Welcome to the real world!

9.

WHAT ABOUT THE VICTIMS?

Of all the lawsuits filled thus far, the most legitimate seems to be that filed on behalf of Catholic priest Florian Gall by his sister Lucille Gall, who, ironically, is also a nurse. It was his death that led to Charles Cullen's arrest in the first place.

Aside from charging that Somerset Medical Center didn't check Cullen's background, the toxicology tests' provide evidence that the presence of digoxin allegedly was covered up by the hospital. Instead, they noted the cause of death on the death certificate as "natural," which is what Lucille Gall had first thought. And Somerset's reputation wasn't helped any when Dennis Miller, its chief executive, said on television that the hospital was not negligent in hiring Cullen, a statement he later repeated in testimony before a state senate committee in Trenton. Technically, according to Miller, the hospital had checked Cullen's references but nothing negative came up. Miller and others at the hospital learned nothing, in fact, until Cullen was arrested and it came out that he had been the subject of numerous investigations, including two for homicide. But while Somerset denied there was a cover-up, the New Jersey Department of Health and Senior Services had already fined them $5,000 anyway. They are contesting the fine.

The son of Frances Shipman has also filed a wrongful death suit in Superior Court. The eighty-one-year-old Frances, again a former nurse, died at Somerset Medical on June 3. Besides naming Charles Cullen and the hospital, earlier hospitals where Cullen worked are also named. Kathleen Roberts, a spokesperson for Somerset Medical, said they have no comment on the suit since they have not seen a copy of the filing.

Finally, in Pennsylvania, five families are suing hospitals. Four patients—Debra Shachter; Marilyn Hall and Loretta Keller, both sixty-six; and eighty-three-year-old Virginia Buttillo—died at St. Luke's. The fifth, Ottomar Schramm, died at Easton Hospital. Neither St. Luke's nor Easton has yet to comment on the cases.

10.

OTHER CASES OF
NURSES WHO KILL

GENENE ANN JONES

It is hard to imagine anything worse than a mother or father handing over a child to a murderer. Or maybe an elderly parent or beloved spouse. Yet that's what has happened in some hospitals. Whenever we leave a loved one in the care of a hospital, we are assured that he or she will be cared for properly and be safe. Sometimes, unhappily, a starched uniform may clothe a mindless killer. The following is one of those stories.

In 1982, Dr. Kathleen Holland decided to open a clinic for children in her hometown of Kerrville, Texas. One of the first people she hired was a licensed nurse named Genene Ann Jones. Jones had previously worked at Bexar County Medical Center Hospital.

Things started off well enough, and the clinic began attracting patients. But something was not quite right. In the first sixty days, seven children had unexpected seizures while at the clinic. Each was rushed by ambulance to nearby Sip Peterson Hospital, and each recovered. While everyone was distressed about the seizures, Dr. Holland didn't suspect anything was wrong. But the staff at Sip Peterson did, and they began to investigate. Then fifteen-month-old Chelsea McClellan had a seizure and like the other children before her was rushed to the hospital, but instead of being saved she died. Holland and the McCellans were devastated, especially since Chelsea hadn't been all that ill. Peterson staff now were convinced that something was amiss.

Genene Jones earlier had reported a bottle of succinylcholine, a powerful muscle relaxant, was lost. Then, three weeks later, she found it. When Dr. Holland inspected it, she noticed that the cap was missing and the rubber membrane covering the bottle's mouth had punctures in it. Alarmed, she fired Jones on the spot. Holland then discovered the bottle mostly contained saline solution, that the succinylcholine had been drawn out. The horror of this drug is that it paralyzes the victim but leaves him or her fully conscious yet unable to speak or move. One dies wide awake but frozen.

Kathleen Holland reported what she knew to authorities. They decided to look into Jones's time at Bexar County Medical, and they found that there had been forty-seven suspicious deaths of children over the four-year period she was there. In February 1983, a grand jury was convened to look into the Bexar deaths while a second grand jury looked into the death of Chelsea McClellan. McClellan's body was exhumed and her tissue tested. Her death appeared to have been caused by succinylcholine. Genene Jones was charged with two counts of murder, and a wrongful death suit was filed by Chelsea's parents. Dr. Holland was also named in the suit.

Yet anyone who knew Genene Jones was not all that surprised. She could be aggressive at times, had betrayed many friends over the years, and often resorted to lies to manipulate others. And she was suspicious of everyone around her. Sadly, she had a brother who died in an accident when he was fourteen years old, which only added to her insecurity. And while she claimed she wanted to have children, the two she did have she'd left in the care of her adoptive mother. From all the signs, perhaps people around Jones should have expected some kind of bizarre ending.

In the midst of Genene Jones's bitter life, the one bright light for her was doctors—male doctors. They were wonderful, powerful men. She had given up being a beautician and trained to be a nurse just to be near them and their world. After graduation, she landed her first hospital job but was fired after only eight months for overstepping her authority and because a patient complained of her abusive treatment. Then she was hired on the intensive care unit of the pediatric ward at Bexar. Her colleagues there almost immediately saw her as awkward, pushy, and sexually needy.

Genene Jones's work at Bexar was not very good, although she willingly put in long hours, and even though her aggressive behavior might have justified dismissal the head nurse liked her and backed her up, which made her feel more powerful than her colleagues. Still, Jones seemed dismayed when the first child died. Later, prosecutors would charge that she had developed a heroine complex, that she reveled in letting a child come close to death and then leaping in at the last moment to try and save it.

In retrospect, it seems odd that Kathleen Holland would have hired Genene Jones in the first place. In fact, Bexar County

Medical staff had warned her against it. But Holland thought people were just picking on Jones for some reason and hadn't give her a fair chance. That mistake cost Holland her career, her marriage, and, worst of all, the life of one of her patients.

In the end, Genene Jones was convicted of murder after mounting an unsuccessful insanity defense and was sentenced to a hundred-plus years in prison. Bexar County Medical settled a wrongful death suit with the McClellans, fired Jones's friend on staff, and destroyed all records of her service there.

DONALD HARVEY

With Donald Harvey, it all began when he was eighteen years old. Starting in May 1970, and for the next ten months, he was an orderly at Marymount Hospital in London, Kentucky. Working there immediately struck a chord inside him of belonging.

To Harvey, the hospital was divided into two camps: those in pain and those trying to relieve it. He quickly empathized with the suffering of the very young and the very old, and he identified with those trying to alleviate that suffering. With no special training, he hit on a way to end the suffering altogether. Simple, direct, and within his power, he would simply kill patients.

The quickest way to do this, he decided, was to smother them, and he did just that with a pillow. He smothered a dozen or more victims, in the process discovering something else: since death is an everyday thing in a hospital, and as long as he didn't make a mess of it, he could get away with it.

Then for some reason Donald Harvey got sidetracked and committed a burglary, got caught, fined, and decided to go a whole new direction by joining the Air Force. It didn't work out, and when he got out a year later he worked as a nurse's aide in various hospitals: Cardinal Hill and Good Samaritan in Lexington, and the VA center in Cincinnati. There, he eventually worked a number of different jobs over the next ten years, including one as an autopsy assistant. It was then that he became the lover of another autopsy assistant, who, it turned out, was having sex with corpses after hours. Harvey's last link to the real world had finally gotten away from him, as had his mind.

One has to wonder about Donald Harvey's tendencies, with his bringing home of tissue samples that some say he used in occult rituals. Whatever those tendencies, they stimulated his urge to kill, and he took the lives of about fifteen more patients. Along the way, he added poison to his repertoire, even joking about it at the time.

Then, in 1985, Donald Harvey was caught with a pistol in the Cincinnati Medical Center, which of course was forbidden. He was carrying a paperback biography of serial killer Charles Sobhraj at the time, possibly to get ideas. He was forced to resign, but he soon found another job at Drake Memorial Hospital, and was back to his old tricks. This time, it is estimated that he murdered some twenty-three patients before being arrested in April 1987. He had been injecting victims with arsenic or cyanide or just plain old petroleum-based cleanser, choosing some of his victims by occult means, chanting over fingernail clipping or strands of hair placed on a homemade altar.

RICHARD ANGELO

In the 1970s, Richard Angelo became known as the Long Island "Angel of Death." A former Eagle Scout who longed to continue performing good deeds, and wanted people to appreciate just how heroic he was, Angelo joined the local volunteer fire department and became an emergency room medical technician. He was twenty-six years old and full of enthusiasm.

At Long Island's busy Good Samaritan Hospital, Angelo was what is known as a "charge nurse," and he had plenty of opportunity to charge about importantly. He loved the crises, the excitement, the more the merrier. And, as always, he especially liked it if he was praised for saving a patient. His zeal apparently led him to generate his own emergencies: he would inject patients with a paralyzing drug, then inject a second drug to save them. Trouble was, some of the patients died.

Richard Angelo killed his first victim, John Fisher, by injecting drugs into his IV tube. When Fisher began to experience problems breathing, Angelo rushed in to save him, but he was too late. Fisher quickly fell into critical condition and died.

Over the months, as Angelo continued on his mission, he was able to save most patients most of the time, but not all of them. Prosecutors estimated that he killed ten people in all. One of his intended victims, Geralano Kucich, fortunately had been alert enough to recognize Angelo's behavior as strange, and his reporting of the would-be hero led to Angelo's arrest and conviction. Kucich had become suspicious when he saw Angelo add something to his IV, and he hit the call button as soon as Angelo left the room. He told the nurse who responded to the call that he had seen a bearded man tampering with his IV, and his description led to Richard Angelo. A urine sample from Kucich tested positive for Pavulon and Anectine, which had not been prescribed for him. When police searched Angelo's apartment, they found vials of both. It was then that he confessed his desire to "create a situation" and he was arrested. He also confessed to overdosing other patients, and the bodies of all ten of his victims were exhumed. All showed traces of drugs that induce paralysis.

Richard Angelo explained that he wanted to induce respiratory distress or some other condition so that "through my intervention or suggested intervention I could look like I knew what I was doing." Up until that time, he had always felt "inadequate," he had had "no confidence in myself."

This Angel of Death was charged with numerous counts of second-degree murder, which carried the added proviso of "depraved indifference." He went to trial in 1989, pleading temporary insanity—specifically, that he did not understand the nature or consequences of his actions. In his defense, psychologists testified that Angelo suffered from multiple personality disorder: he did not recognize the risk to the patients at the time, and afterward he was completely unaware of what he had done.

When Richard Angelo agreed to take a polygraph test, it showed he was telling the truth about how he felt at the time his victims died. In rebuttal, two mental health experts testifying for the prosecution agreed that Angelo indeed suffered from personality disorder, but that that did not preclude him from know right from wrong or from knowing the risk he was taking.

Following extensive testimony, a jury convicted Angelo of two counts of second-degree murder, one count of second-degree manslaughter, one count of criminally negligent homicide, and six counts of assault. He was sentenced to sixty-one years to life. The patients he poisoned, of course, all got death.

ORVILLE LYNN MAJORS

A callous attitude, especially toward senior citizens, seems to be the reason that nurse Orville Majors took it upon himself to kill many of the patients in his care when he worked at Vermillion County Hospital in Clinton, Indiana. When he joined the staff of the small fifty-six-bed facility in 1993, an average of twenty-five people died there each year. By 1994, the death toll had jumped to an alarming 101. Sixty-seven had happened during the preceding six months, sixty-three on Majors's shift.

During his twenty-two month at Vermillion, 147 died, the majority of them on his shift. Although Majors seemed unaware that people might question such figures, one of his supervisors did just that and began to investigate. As a result, Majors's license was suspended in 1995, and the death rate at the hospital returned to normal. He then became the subject of an expensive investigation, during which fifteen bodies were exhumed and tested for epinephrine and potassium chloride. Most of the victims had experienced an alarming rise in blood pressure just before their hearts stopped, and six showed traces of one drug or the other. The investigation would eventually look into a total of sixty deaths. A search of Majors's home turned up syringes, needles, and vials of epinephrine and potassium chloride. Vials of potassium chloride were also found in a van owned by his parents which he drove.

Orville Majors was charged with six counts of murder, although he is suspected of having committed upwards of 130. During his lengthy trial, seventy witnesses took the stand, and they repeatedly spoke of his cold attitude toward patients. Some reported seeing him administer injections, something he was not authorized to do, and those receiving the injections later died. One witness said that when patients died, Majors would shrug and make some casual remark, and another witness, a former roommate, testified that Majors had no use for the elderly, once declaring that they should be gassed. Statistically speaking, it was also pointed out that patients were 43 percent more likely to die at Vermillion when Majors was on duty.

In his own defense, Orville Lynn Majors blamed his killing spree solely on the effects of long shifts and overtime hours worked. In October 1999, he was convicted on all six counts and sentenced to life.

LEONORA PEREZ AND FILIPINA NARCISO

In the mid-1970s, the FBI and Veterans Administration tried in vain to convict two nurses from the Philippines, Lenora Perez and Filipina Narciso, both in their early thirties at the time, of murder because of the exceptionally high death rate at the VA hospital in Ann Arbor, Michigan, where they worked. Evidence was insufficient to convict, however, and the killer or killers of some forty veterans, all of whom had died of sudden unexplained respiratory failure, remain at large.

The investigation established that eight men had died from an overdose of Pavulon. In time, Perez and Narciso became the focus of investigators—they had been on duty in each case. They were charged with murder, and witnesses, including victims' family members, testified that they had seen the two in the vicinity or actually in the victims' rooms on the days in question. But prosecutors had nothing but circumstantial evidence to go on, and again it proved too little for a conviction. Since the nurses had not actually been seen administering Pavulon or using it in any way, the judge threw out the murder charge against Perez at her trial, and, after a thirteen-week trial, Narciso was acquitted of murder too. Additional convictions for conspiracy and poisoning were thrown out on appeal.

As of this writing, Leonora Perez and Filipina Narciso are free and probably still working in a hospital somewhere.

AMY ARCHER-GILLIAN

The motives of the self-appointed executioner vary from one twisted mind to the next, but some are fueled simply by the desire for money no matter what it takes to get it. Doctors and nurses, trusted by their patients, and usually with no one second-guessing their work, have been known to do a patient ill out of greed. Although there are no records kept on such duplicity, it is believed that many who have gained from their patients' deaths then went on to live out their years without ever being suspected of any but the best of intentions regarding their patients. Every so often, however, a case emerges.

Take the story of Amy Archer-Gilligan. In 1901, she advertised that she was opening a nursing home for the aged in Newington, Connecticut. While her eventual patients came to love her, calling her "Sister Amy," the money was none too plentiful. So she came up with a scheme.

In 1907, Archer-Gilligan opened the Archer Home for the Elderly and Infirm a few miles down the road in Windsor. She asked patients for $1,000 up front to ensure lifetime care. While they happily complied, they never considered that she might shorten their lifespans for her own gain. Nor did Dr. Howard King, a friend, ever question that patients had died in her facility of old age, taking Archer-Gilligan's word for it and routinely signing death certificates.

In reality, once the thousand dollars was in hand, the patients would be smothered or poisoned.

Forty people died at Sister Amy's fourteen-bed facility between 1911 and 1916. Both of her husbands died, too, one within a year of his wedding to this fatally charismatic woman. Authorities finally became suspicious, and, as part of their investigation, a police officer posing as a patient entered the home. Archer-Gilligan told him about the lifetime care plan, and of the wonderful care he would be receiving, and he paid. But while he was there, he also collected enough evidence to charge her with fraud. And he found evidence of foul play. The bodies of some of the deceased patients and her second husband were exhumed and high levels of arsenic were found in a number of them. When Dr. King was questioned about his incorrect notations on the death certificates, he said they were correct, that someone had planted the arsenic, that Sister Amy had been framed.

Amy Archer-Gilligan was eventually charged with six counts of murder. Her defense was that she was a devout Christian woman and that her faith would never have allowed her to commit such crimes. But experts testified that the number of deaths for a nursing facility the size of hers should have been more like eight or ten a year and not forty-eight. The jury convicted her of the most recent death only and she was given life. Instead, Archer-Gilligan was institutionalized in a hospital for the insane.

ANNA MARIE HAHN

"Nurse" Anna Marie Hahn concocted her own plan for getting rich. She had come to America from Germany in 1929 and settled in Cincinnati. Before long, she befriended several wealthy elderly men, offering them health care, and they rewarded her by naming her in their wills. In a matter of only a few years, Hahn was rich herself: she had inherited one man's estate outright, and she had taken a number of items from the homes of two others who had died.

The police learned that the deaths of the last two men were unexpected, however, and their relatives were suspicious. The body of the second to die was exhumed, and it was determined that he had been poisoned with arsenic, which was then followed by a potent purgative. Upon searching Hahn's home, numerous poisons were found. Other exhumations followed, and she was eventually put on trial for three murders.

During the trial, even Hahn's own husband testified against her. She had attempted to persuade him to take out a large life insurance policy on himself and name her as beneficiary. When he had refused, he had begun suffering stomach cramps. Even if she couldn't get money out of him, he still wasn't worth keeping around.

Convicted, Anna Marie Hahn had the dubious distinction of being the first woman to die in Ohio's electric chair. Until the day she died, she insisted she was innocent. She did agree, however, that she was indeed a swindler and a thief.

KRISTEN GILBERT: KILLING FOR FUN

For whatever reason, history has shown that there are many more men who become mass murderers or serial killers than women. Until recently, only two women in the United States, in fact, had been tried, convicted, and executed for this crime. Strangely, both were in the same year, 1953.

More recently, thirty-three-year-old Kristen Gilbert, who lived in

Massachusetts, where witch hunts were once the norm, came very close to be the first woman executed there since 1789. In March 2001, she became the focus of a federal investigation that put her squarely on the path to death row. Traditionally against the death penalty, Massachusetts citizens were in a somewhat unforgiving frame of mind when the details of this woman's crimes came out. The fact that she was a nurse only emphasized their heinous nature more.

It all began in 1996 when three nurses who worked with Kristen Gilbert on Ward C of the Veterans Affairs Medical Center in Northampton began to wonder at the unusual number of patients who were dying from cardiac arrest over a relatively short period of time. The three took their concerns to the hospital administration, believing that there might be a killer working on the ward.

Gilbert, the divorced mother of two sons, then seven and ten years of age, gave every appearance of being a well-trained, hardworking, completely normal employee. Strangely, though, it was on her shift that so many patients died from heart failure: four had died directly under her care, and three others had come close to dying. At the same time, there was a sudden unexplained shortage on the ward of epinephrine, a synthetic adrenaline formulation that is used to stimulate the heart when it shows signs of failure. Even more damning, Gilbert was observed by many as being almost ecstatic in the excitement surrounding a cardiac emergency.

The hospital administration notified federal investigators of their suspicions and investigators in turn had the bodies of the most recently deceased patients under Gilbert's care exhumed. Careful toxicological analysis verified that indeed there were high levels of epinephrine present in tissue samples. Checking patient medical records, none had ever had the drug prescribed to them—there was no reason, in other words, that the drug should be present in any of them.

A rather curious incident happened about this same time: someone called in a bomb threat to the hospital's main desk— Kristen Gilbert was soon convicted of the lesser charge of attempting to divert attention away from a federal investigation. After being charged with and convicted of making the call, she served fifteen months and was ordered to undergo psychiatric counseling. It was at this time that she came under scrutiny for the much more serious charge of murder, and prosecutor William Welch began carefully compiling enough evidence to bring Gilbert back to court and convict her.

It seems that Kristen Gilbert had been having an affair with hospital security staff member James Perrault. Part of his job description entailed responding immediately to any emergency call on the ward. How convenient for Gilbert, who was observed flirting with him on a number of occasions. Welch would later accuse her of actually killing a patient just so she could leave work early to keep a date with Perrault.

Their affair long over, James Perrault took the stand and testified against Kristen Gilbert. He told the court that although he didn't take it seriously at the time, she had actually mentioned to him that she had killed several patients by giving them injections of epinephrine. Several other comments by her only made him think she might be a menace if what she said were really true. But, alas, he didn't believe her, and he did nothing.

Kathy Rix, another nurse, suspecting something was not right, noted one afternoon that there were three vials of epinephrine on the shelf in storage. Soon after that, there was a cardiac emergency on the ward and when Rix rushed to storage she found that all three were gone. At the same time, she notice three broken epinephrine vials in a needle disposal container nearby.

Another damaging piece of testimony came from a different nurse who told of hearing the first victim crying out "Stop! . . . Stop! . . . You're killing me!" when Gilbert was in the room with the patient. And Bonnie Bledsoe, yet another nurse, who is prone to asthma, was suffering an attack when Gilbert chanced by and offered her some adrenaline she just happened to have in her pocket.

In Gilbert's defense, lawyer David Hoose observed that no one actually saw his client injecting any of the victims. And, besides, these people were quite ill already, people die in hospitals all the time, how could anyone blame this innocent nurse? By his argument, James Perrault had turned against his ex-lover because of romantic disappointment and not because Gilbert had actually confessed to anything. Hoose suggested she had been very angry at Perrault and actually was trying to scare him with her wild talk. In other words, he was making a mountain out of a molehill.

To explain away the missing epinephrine, Hoose was quick to blame anyone who might have a drug problem as taking the vials. He then characterized the toxicology report as shoddy at best—that by its very nature toxicology's an inexact science. Grasping at straws, he finally tried to throw suspicion on a well-known federal prosecutor by claiming he wanted to convince and execute Gilbert, a white woman, just to balance out the scales of justice that are weighed so heavily in society against the black man.

Kristen Gilbert was found guilty of three counts of first-degree murder, one count of second-degree murder, and two counts of attempted murder. Because the crimes were committed on federal territory, and because the victims were so much at the mercy of the woman that killed them, that and her heartlessly cruel attitude at trial, the government sought the death penalty. To the dismay of many, she only got life.

GWENDOLYN GAIL GRAHAM AND CATHERINE MAY WOOD: SEX IN THE WOODS

Gwendolyn Gail Graham, twenty-three, and Catherine May Wood, twenty-four, worked together in a live-in nursing facility, the Alpine Manor Nursing Home, in Walker, Michigan. In 1987, these two lovers decided to make sex and death bedmates. Wood, who had been married for a short time before meeting Graham, her immediate supervisor at Alpine Manor, suffered emotionally after the recent breakup of her marriage and gained a tremendous amount of weight. Looking for any kind of closeness, she found Graham's easy friendship a welcome relief and the two became involved.

Gwendolyn Graham made the first mention of murder between them. As lovers, they enhanced their orgasms by practicing the bizarre technique known as "sexual asphyxia," so Wood thought Graham was just joking when she suggested that murder could also enhance their pleasure. At the same time, linking pleasure to death evolved into shades of cruelty and sadism. Just talking about killing brought both to greater heights of arousal.

The actual killing began in January of that year and continued for the next three months. They made a macabre game of choosing elderly victims whose names began with a letter from the word murder—the "murder game," Graham called it. Wood would then stand guard as Graham attempted to smother several bedridden women. Attempted, because the intended victims turned out to be much stronger than expected and were able to fend her off. Strangely, none ever registered a complaint with the hospital administration or outside authorities. Quite the opposite, in fact: most of the patients thought the world of the two women.

Their first success was the killing a patient who suffered from Alzheimer's and wasn't able to fight back—Graham smothered her with a wet washcloth. After that, the killings came at fairly regular intervals over the next several weeks.

There were times that the very act of killing incited such lust that Graham and Wood would slip into a vacant room to enjoy themselves. Then Graham began taking personal items from the victims, including jewelry—and in some cases even false teeth—just to have something to remind her of the event and re-create the arousal she felt while killing. When the two, as part of their duties, washed the victims' bodies, they would become excited all over again. As time went on, the two became bolder, on several occasions even announcing to coworkers that they had been murdering some of the patients, which aroused them even further. These coworkers already considered the pair a little strange, so they took the confessions as just another quirk of personality, a sick joke at best. Graham went so far as to show three of them her collection of pilfered odds and ends and still no one questioned either of them or attempted to stop them.

At some point, Gwendolyn Graham decided she wanted Catherine Wood to become more involved in the actual killing, and she insisted that Wood perform the next one to prove her love for her. Wood balked at the idea, and, when pressured further by

Graham, had herself transferred to another shift to escape the harassment. About this time, Graham found herself a new lover, then pulled up stakes and left Michigan to take a new position taking care of infants at a hospital in Texas.

With Gwendolyn Graham gone, a terrified Catherine Wood could no longer live with their secret and confessed everything to her ex-husband. Even knowing that she was telling the truth, he took over a year to get up the courage to tell the authorities.

During the women's killing spree, there were some forty deaths in the home, eight of which were unusual enough to attract the authorities' attention. Narrowing the number of victims down to five, they placed both women under arrest and booked them on suspicion of murder.

Catherine Wood, still reeling from the part she'd played, and in return for a reduced sentence of twenty to forty years, turned state's evidence and implicated her former lover. She explained the reason she decided to come clean was that shortly after Graham started working with infants in Texas she told her she just wanted to "take one of the babies and smash it up against the window."

For her part, Gwendolyn Graham, hoping to reduce her own sentence, claimed her father had repeatedly molested her as a child, but there was no proof of this and her defense argument was thrown out. Graham's lawyer also played the jilted lover card, claiming Wood blew the whistle on Graham and made false statements against her just because Graham had run off to Texas without her.

The jury believed Catherine May Wood, and Gwendolyn Gail Graham was convicted on five counts of first-degree murder and one count of attempted murder. Wood also made a sworn statement that there had been five additional attempts to smother patients. As it was, Graham was sentenced top six consecutive life sentences with no possibility of parole.

In all of the above cases, and in others just like them, people who take advantage of the disadvantaged they care for just to satisfy their own personal needs are certainly depraved. They defy the honor code of trust placed in them as caregivers. Is it because of horrible treatment they suffered at the hands of others in the past that they do what they do, or is it simply that they want to be domineering and all-powerful? Whatever the motive, they take the lives of their innocent victims and erode the faith we place in the medical community.

THE TORONTO HOSPITAL CASE:
AN UNSOLVED MYSTERY

In 1980 and 1981, the Hospital for Sick Children in Toronto sustained a disproportionately high number of patient deaths: the mortality rate was six times what it had been in 1978 and 1979. Sadly, only after twenty children had died, many unexpectedly and unexplained, did nurses at the facility report to the doctors that something seemed amiss. The hospital conducted an investigation but found nothing wrong, so nothing was done.

Finally, a baby girl who died unexpectedly underwent an autopsy. Surprisingly, there were substantial traces of digoxin in her tissue, certainly enough to be fatal. Two other suspicious cases were looked into and they, too, showed high concentrations of digoxin.

Three nurses working on the pediatric ward of the hospital were immediately placed on administrative leave. Their lockers were searched and their backgrounds checked. But while they were on leave, yet another infant suffered a digoxin overdose.

It was then that nurse Susan Nelles was arrested on suspicion of murder. All the infants had died while she was on duty. Further, several nurses had seen her making what they called "funny faces," although no one seemed to know what that meant. Yet, while she too was on leave several nurses began complaining that the hospital food tasted "funny," and it was later discovered that there were traces of several different chemicals in it—something that has never been explained.

In July 1982, a discovery hearing was convened, from which it was determined that Susan Nelles may have been responsible for as many as sixteen infants' deaths during the previous year. But after a four-month trial, nothing concrete could be leveled against her. The judge then praised Nelles for her professional behavior and skills as a child care specialist, and dismissed the case.

In a final attempt to try to find out what really happened, the Hospital for Sick Children asked the Centers for Disease Control (CDC) to conduct an independent investigation. The CDC concluded that a number of deaths had indeed been the result of murder, that some were merely suspicious, and that some could not be explained at all. And while attention has been paid to this mystery sporadically over the past twenty years, no resolution has been forthcoming.

11.

THE SILENT MINORITY: MALE NURSES

One group particularly affected by the Charles Cullen scandal is the relatively small fraternity of health professional whose struggle with image is already so well known that it's even the subject of a recent movie comedy: the male nurse. Nurse Jerry Lucas cringed when he heard about Cullen because his actions seemed to reinforce another, much uglier stereotype: even though males account for only about 6 percent of nurses in the United States, they seem to dominate the ranks of nurses who kill. Lucas, also the publisher of Male Nurse magazine, says, "If we're not the angel of death, we're sex-crazed maniacs or failed doctors. It hurts us when we get a story like this out there because we're such a small minority, so it takes center stage." In the last twenty-five years at the Medical Center of Southern Indiana, where he works, seventeen nurses or nurse's aides have been charged with murder but only seven were men. He thinks it's just as likely that there are as many female killers pursuing their craft as male.

Lawyer and San Francisco State school of nursing director Beatrice Crofts Yorker believes that men are more likely to get caught than women, however, and Katherine Ramsland, who teaches forensic psychology at DeSales University in Pennsylvania, agrees. "Part of it is our gender bias. We're much more reluctant to think of women as potential killers, so there may be more women out there who aren't being caught." Nurses like Kristen Gilbert, she adds, are better at covering their tracks.

Still, both sexes think it is easier for men to kill in a hospital setting, and men may feel more driven to prove they're not just failed doctors, that they are capable of being in charge. In fact, it is generally agreed that male nurses often are granted more authority than female by colleagues and patients alike. It's easier for them to move around the hospital and do things and not be challenged by others.

Another problem is a growing shortage of nurses, regardless of gender, which means we may see less qualified nurses overall in years to come. Jerry Lucas sums up the situation as follows: "With such a nursing shortage, I could quit a job and twenty minutes later be employed again. Hospitals are not looking for credentials. They're looking for a live body to put into that nursing hole, and what you get is these kinds of kooks [like Charles Cullen]."

12.

THE FUTURE:

CHANGING THE SYSTEM?

What can be done to stop nurses who kill? Obviously, there are bound to be limits and conflicting points of view about what the best option may be. More nurses, better training, and better screening may help to weed out undesirables, but where will the money come from to do it? Higher taxes or deeper cuts in other government services are possible, but who would vote to increase taxes or cut firemen, policemen, and teachers' salaries, or reduce money for libraries or road improvements?

Can the system for licensing nurses and tracking them from one job to the next be improved? One of the weaknesses of the present system is its cloak of secrecy. Although Charles Cullen was fired at least six times, quit three times on his own, and several times attempted to commit suicide, nothing in his official record would indicate it. Now everybody wants to change things, wants to protect the public from another Charles Cullen, but how are we going to do it, and at what cost?

New Jersey and Pennsylvania politicians were quick to weigh in on the case. "There was, I believe, a breakdown in the system," said State Senator Joseph Vitale stating the obvious, "because it took so long and so many people had to die before this person was captured." Some officials call for a national file that any hospital can access to check an employee's history. Ironically, there already is such a file in existence, but few know how to use it, and few hospitals are able or all that willing to report on staff.

What about the legal liabilities if changes are made? Can a bad report on the record constitute libel and be grounds for a lawsuit? Who would want to risk legal action, with all its attendant aggravation and expense? Not the hospital, certainly, nor its stockholders and staff. Should the government take over the records system? But, again, who pays?

Consider, for a minute, something as simple as installing closed-circuit television cameras in every hospital room. Immediately, you're dealing with a Fourth Amendment issue: "The right of the people to be secure in their persons, houses, papers, and effects, against unreasonable searches and seizures, shall not be violated and no warrants shall issue, but upon probable cause, supported by oath or affirmation, and particularly describing the place to be searched, and the person or things to be seized." Meaning, evidence seized in violation of the Fourth Amendment is not admissible in court. Even a videotape of a nurse killing a patient may not qualify. You need a search warrant to set up the camera in the first place, or you need to prove there was no "reasonable expectation of privacy" on the part of the victim or killer. One special circumstance might be that the suspect will destroy evidence or kill the patient imminently. But then staff might clog the courts seeking warrants or approvals. Impractical, yes, but not impossible: some courts have allowed cameras on the application of just one individual.

Gary Carter, president of the New Jersey Hospital Association, makes the point that with hundreds of thousands of nurses, doctors, and medical personnel at work every day, realistically one "cannot always prevent a criminal act." But that doesn't mean that we should accept murder as an everyday part of our health care system.

Nurses want to protect patients, but they need protection themselves. Ann Twomey, an officer of the Health Professionals and Allied Employees group, says, "Nurses who do report unsafe practices or suspicious activity must be protected from recriminations." Hospitals want protection, too. Right now, they protect themselves with a code of silence to avoid lawsuits. For example, New York hospitals are required to file reports, which become public, on their most serious mistakes. But from May 2000 to June 2003, only three were filed. One unfiled report was on a twelve-year-old boy who was mistakenly given three months' worth of chemotherapy in three days.

The case of Charles Cullen is a shocker, no doubt about it. But, in reality, crimes like his are reported all the time. For example, the January 22 issue of U.S. News & World Report carried the story of beloved English doctor Harold Shipman whose elderly patient died suddenly leaving him all of her money. He was eventually found guilty of injecting fifteen women with lethal doses of heroin. Police estimated the figure is more like three hundred. Yet his still-living patients organized a support group for him. One person who did not join the group was the coroner, who discovered that Shipman had killed her grandmother.

Some people think Harold Shipman is the most lethal serial killer ever in the field of medicine. Yet there are contenders to that title in America, U.S. News goes on. There is angel of death Efren Saldivar, or relatively recent cases like Michael Swango, who murdered four patients in New York and Ohio, or Orville Majors, who was found guilty of murdering six. Perversely, Majors's coworkers used to bet on who would be the next to die while he was on duty. And of course, there's Charles Cullen.

Clearly, there are angels of death out there, and clearly there are no surefire ways to stop them. Overwhelmingly, health care workers are dedicated to saving lives, and they need to be supported and protected just as much as every patient and family does. People need to learn about the problem in order to muster support to remedy it. Until then, more will die needlessly.

And just how do we know this? In 1999, a study released by the National Institutes for Medicine in Washington, D.C., concluded that ninety-eight thousand Americans die each year from medical mistakes that are preventable. In other words, about twenty-five patients have died around the country in the time it took most people to read this book.

END NOTES

CHAPTER ONE: THE BIZARRE LIFE OF CAREGIVING MURDERER CHARLES CULLEN

as many as 500 deaths... Michele McPhee, William Sherman, Tony Sclafani, Richard T. Peinciak, "What Makes Sicko Tick," *New York Daily News*, December 21, 2003

Cullen's Instability

attempted suicide at least.... Richard Perez Pena, David Kocieniewski and Jason George, "Death on the Night Shift," *The New York Times*, February 29, 2004

He stuck me... Ibid

She looked green...Ibid

The End Begins and Other Nurses Act

Somebody killed him...Ibid

The Confession

I don't want to contest...McDermott, Joe, "Murder Charge For Nurse; He Admits Killing 30-40," *The Morning Call*, December 16, 2003

only charged with... AP in *Courier News*, February 18, 2003, Somerville, New Jersey

Reviewing and Analyzing Killing Caregivers

The killings are quiet... John J. Goldman, "The Ripple Effect of One Confession," *Los Angeles Times*, December 22, 2003

They are not obviously violent... Ibid

These people tend to be serial killers... Ibid

Glendale and Other Parallel Cases

We had too much work... Paul Lieberman, "Graveyard Shift," *Los Angeles Times*, April 29, 2002

When I was at my wits' end... Ibid

unusual number of orders... John J. Goldman, "The Ripple Effect of One Confession," *Los Angeles Times*, December 22, 2003

CHAPTER TWO: HOSPITAL KILLERS AS A SERIOUS THREAT

Some killers use that... Eric Wahlgren, "Hospital Killers Race But Real Threat in U.S.; Cases Show Detection Difficult," *Los Angeles Daily News*, April 5, 1998

Our members are wondering... Ibid

Efren Saldivar helped a patient die fast... Donna Huffakeer, *Los Angeles Daily News*, March 7, 1999

CHAPTER THREE: THE ROLE OF NURSES IN ACTION

You'd take such good care... Ann Wlazelek, Matt Assad, "Nurses' Warnings Unable To Stop Trail Of Death," *The Morning Call*, February 15, 2004

They said he'd come on... Ibid

Everyone is afraid... Ibid

Without toxicology how do you know... Ibid

His nursing licenses...Richard Perez Pena, David Kocieniewski and Jason George, "Death on the Night Shift," *The New York Times*, February 29, 2004

CHAPTER FIVE: THE WHY OF SERIAL MURDERS

Is It Mercy Killing?

The classic cases... Joyce Howard Price, "Nurses, Multiple Killings Linked in Troubling Trend," *Washington Times*, December 7, 1998

Bull... Ibid

particulary drawn to... Ibid

get into problems with... Ibid

Unfortunately, when something... Ibid

The majority of the perpetrators... Ibid

CHAPTER SIX: ARE LAWYERS TO BLAME?

InjuryBoard.com provides the general public... "About Injury Board.com," www.injuryboard.com, 2004

CHAPTER SEVEN: IS A WEAK NURSE TRACKING SYSTEM TO BLAME?

technology didn't fail them... David B. Caruso, AP On Line via COMTEX, December 21, 2003

Unfortunately, you have bureaucrats... Ibid

Hospital risk management... Ibid

CHAPTER EIGHT: THE FLYING LAWSUITS

St. Luke's is increasingly appalled... Scott Kraus, "St. Luke's: Cullen didn't kill woman," *The Morning Call*, January 9, 2004

CHAPTER TEN: OTHER CASES OF NURSES WHO KILL

Richard Angelo

through my intervention...Tom Demoretcky, "Crime in the Suburbs," *New York Newsday*, June 20, 1998

Kristen Gilbert: Killing for Fun

Stop... stop... You're killing me... Tom Bell, *Bergen Record*, New Jersey, December 19, 2003

CHAPTER ELEVEN: THE SILENT MINORITY: MALE NURSES

If we're not... Tina Susman, "Their Honorable Vocation Dishonored," *Newsday*, January 13, 2004

Part of it is our gender bias... Ibid

With such a nursing shortage... Ibid

CHAPTER TWELVE: THE FUTURE: CHANGING THE SYSTEM

because it took so long... John P. McAlpin, AP On Line, December 22, 2003

cannot always prevent a criminal act... "N.J. Lawmakers Seek Changes in Hospitals," The Associated Press, December 23, 2003

Nurses who do report... Ibid